I0004539

Online Privacy:

An Introduction to TOR Network and Online Security

How to stay anonymous in the Internet

William Rowley

Copyright ©2015 William Rowley
All Rights Reserved

This book or parts thereof may not be reproduced in any form, stored in any
retrieval system, or transmitted in any form be any means-electronic,
mechanical, photocopy, recording, or otherwise-without prior written
permission of the Publisher.

In this book you'll learn:

Conclusion 31

This book is about the Tor browser. It starts by defining what it is, where it is used, how it functions and its origin. The book will guide you on how to install Tor browser on Mac OS X, Linux and Windows. The necessary instructions for each platform are explored.

On reading this book, you will learn about the Exit Nodes in Tor, which mark where the encrypted traffic enters the internet. You will learn how to configure Tor so that it can use a certain country as an exit node. Most people are harassed after using Exit Nodes in Tor.

This book will guide you on how to avoid this. LongLivedPorts in Tor are also explored. You will get to learn what they are, and how to establish long-lived connections such as the one used to chat. On reading this book, you will understand how to protect yourself from fake entry nodes.

You will also learn how to change the frequency with which the routing path is changed in Tor by altering the parameters NewCircuitPeriod, MaxCircuitDirtiness and CircuitIdleTimeout. After reading this book, you will learn how to access the dark internet using Tor and how to create a Tor button on Chrome. The book will also guide you on how to ensure your safety while running Tor on windows. The following topics are discussed:

- Definition
- Getting started with Tor Browser
- Tor Exit Nodes
- TrackHostExists
- LongLivedPorts in Tor
- EntryNodes in Tor
- The Routing Path in Tor
- Accessing Dark Internet using Tor

- Creating a Tor button in Chrome
- Using Tor safely on windows
- Tips while using Tor Browser

Introduction

Many people want to conceal their usage and their location while using the internet. This is what led to the development of the Tor browser which lets users browse anonymously. It works by encrypting the data and concealing the IP address of both the source and destination of the traffic.

People who perform network surveillance or traffic analysis will then be unable to trace what you have done on the internet as well as your location. The browser has gained popularity, particularly among people who want to ensure the privacy and confidentiality of their internet activity.

Chapter 1: Definition

TOR stands for third-generation onion routing. It was developed for anonymous web browsing using encryption techniques. The idea behind this is to hide the usage and location of the user from anyone performing traffic analysis or network surveillance, meaning that the activity of the internet will not be traced back to the user.

Normally, the forms of communication such as online posts, visit to websites, and instant messages are used for tracing actions. Tor will prevent this on your part. With this browser, the privacy and confidentiality of users' communication is highly enhanced. This is achieved by avoiding the monitoring of their internet activity.

Tor employs the use of "encryption routing", whereby encryption is done at the application layer of the communication protocol stack. The data and the IP address are all encrypted, meaning that one can neither read the data being transmitted via the network nor identify the origin or the destination of the data. The process of encryption is performed several times before the encrypted data is sent through a virtual circuit made of multiple Tor relays. At each relay, a layer of encryption is encrypted and the next relay in the circuit is revealed. The innermost layer of the encryption is encrypted by the final relay. However, the IP address of the source is not revealed or even known. Due to the process of concealing the routing information in each and every relay in the Tor circuit, it becomes difficult for people carrying out network surveillance to get any information related to this from any node or relay. For them to defeat this anonymity provided by Tor, they must use other means such as the exploitation of a vulnerable form of software on a user's computer.

Tor was first used by the US Navy for the purpose of concealing sensitive communication. Its use has since grown widely, partly because it has become open-source software. Political activists use this browser due to fear of both surveillance and arrest. Other groups which use Tor include business professionals, law enforcement officials, reporters, and whistle-blowers.

However, it is good to note that the use of Tor alone is not enough to guarantee 100% privacy or the confidentiality of your network activity. Malware has been used to successfully attack both networks and browsers. This explains why other means for ensuring privacy and confidentiality of internet activity should be employed alongside Tor if you seek a guarantee of your security.

Chapter 2: Getting started with Tor Browser

The first thing before getting started is to download and install the browser itself onto your computer. The browser supports multiple different languages, different operating systems, and different versions in terms of bits for each operating system. It can run on Mac, Windows and Linux machines.

Instructions for Mac OS X

Begin by downloading the file, and then save it somewhere accessible. Once you click on it, a .dmg file will be opened. If you are running the latest version of OS X, you might be warned that it this file comes from an unidentified developer. To solve this, just press the CTRL key before clicking on it. Choose "open". You should then drag the file which has been included in the Application's folder. You will then have the browser in the language of your choice.

Instructions for Linux

As usual, begin by downloading the Linux version of the browser. To extract it, open the terminal and run the following commands.

For 32-bit version:

tar -xvJf tor-browser-linux32-4.0.6_LANGUAGE.tar.xz

For 64-bit version:

tar -xvJf tor-browser-linux64-4.0.6_LANGUAGE.tar.xz

LANGUAGE should be the language which has been listed in the filename. Once you are done with the above commands, navigate to the browser's directory as follows:

cd tor-browser_LANGUAGE

Again, LANGUAGE is the language which has been listed in the filename. Now it is time to run the browser. Just execute the following script:

. /start-tor-browser

The above command will launch the Tor launcher. This will in turn launch Tor and Firefox will then be launched as well.

Instructions on Windows

The process is simple for Windows. Just download the file and save it somewhere accessible. Double click on the downloaded file and choose "Run". Select the language and the click "Ok". The location chosen should have a minimum of 80 MB free disk space. Save the bundle on the desktop if you don't want to remove it from the computer. Start the installation by clicking on "Install". Wait until the installation process is over. Be patient as it may take some minutes. Once the process is complete, then click on "Finish". This will launch the Tor browser's wizard. After the wizard has appeared, click on "connect". You can also open the folder where you had saved the bundle and then click on "Start Tor Browser". The browser will then open. The only web pages sent via Tor are ones visited by the Tor browser. Note that this will not affect the other browsers such as the Internet Explorer.

Once, you are through with browsing. Just close the Tor browser, making sure that you don't leave behind any open Tor browser window. Once you have done this, Tor will delete all the web pages you have visited as well as all the cookies. This is good for ensuring privacy. If you need to use it again, that is, the browser, just open the usual folder where you saved the bundle and again, click on "Start Tor Browser".

Remember that the purpose of Tor is to conceal the origin of your traffic. It works by encrypting everything in the Tor network. However, the traffic between the Tor network and the final destination is not encrypted. If the data in exchange is too sensitive, then it is recommended that you do this warily, just to be on the safe side. For encryption and authentication purposes, use HTTPS. Other means for doing this can also be put into use.

Chapter 3: Tor Exit Nodes

The exit node marks where the encrypted traffic enters the internet. This means that persons carrying out traffic analysis or network surveillance can take advantage of these and abuse them. Tor relies on numerous exit nodes. Note that these are periodically changed as you continue using the internet. They are usually safe but not monitored. Good internet citizens are responsible for the management of Tor exit nodes.

Configuring Tor to Use a Country as the Exit Node

For certain websites, you can access their services if and only if you are accessing them from specific countries. This relies on the IP address and the system time whether one tries to access these services. These are used to determine your location which establishes whether you can access the services of the website or application. However, it is possible to bypass this restriction. You just have to configure your Tor browser and then you will be able to access these services. You can configure the Tor browser in such a way that the exit node falls in the country where the service is being provided. There servers in specific countries which run the Tor software and function as exit nodes in those locations. Whenever you run the software, an exit node will be automatically assigned to you. However, it is possible to customize the selection of this exit node for your machine, which most people do not know.

In this chapter, we will use a package called Vidalia which is a part of the Tor browser. It has all the programs which can guide you in selecting a specific country when using the Tor browser. Begin by downloading the Tor browser. Once the download is over, just run or install it. After running Vidalia for the first time, the interface will look as follows:

The status of Tor is displayed here. In my case, it is connected to the internet. The rest of the information will assist us in finding servers located in the country that we want. Once you click on view the network, if Tor is running, all the available servers will be displayed. A country flag can be used to sort the servers according to their countries. Performance indicators can also be placed next to these. It is good to note the servers which have the best performance. These should be used as the exit nodes while configuring Tor. Click on the settings and you will find a menu where you can enter the configurations for Tor.

Once you click on browse, a dialogue will be presented to you. Left click the "torrc" file. From the menu, choose "edit". Paste the following lines at the beginning of the configuration:

ExitNodes 1stserver, 2ndserver, 3rdserver
StrictExitNodes 1

Replace the 1st server, 2nd server and 3rd server with the server names you noted from the network display window. To apply the changes, just stop and restart the Tor browser.

If you are using a different browser other than the Tor Browser Bundle, then you need to follow the following step. We should add the http proxy to the browser. If you are using Firefox, click Tools > Options > Advanced Network. You should then choose Settings. Select manual proxy configuration. Set the HTTP proxy to 'localhost' and the port to '8118'. You can then perform a test to confirm whether everything is working correctly. As I'm sure you have noticed, the above procedure is very simple. You will use the exit nodes of your choice rather than using the ones offered by the anonymity service.

Tips to Avoid Harassment while Running an Exit Node

1. Inform the Potential ISP(s) - it is not recommended that you run an exit node using your home internet. Your home connection should only be used for middle or bridge nodes. You should instead find a colo to use. The bandwidth will also be cheaper this way. It is good to choose an ISP who you can trust. Explain to them what it is that you expect. Ask them about the services that they can provide. Finally, inquire more about Tor and why you need it for your internet
2. Obtain a Different IP for the Node- your own traffic should not be routed via this IP. This separation will ensure that DMCA notices and abuse complaints are responded with a boilerplate response. This is contrary to provisions concerning personal information to personal cartels and the cutting of personal communication.
3. Obtain a Reverse DNS for the IP which can be Recognized- knee-jerk reactions which result from DoS kiddies and sysadmins will be largely prevented once we set a good Reverse DNS name for the exit IP.

4. Add a Tor Exit Notice- a notice to indicate that someone is running an exit node should be included. You should also update it regularly.

5. If Available, Get an ARIN Registration- you should consider creating an account with ARIN. You should then create ORG IDs and POC handles for yourself. The next step will be getting an ISP.

6. Reduced Exit Policy is Recommended- you will receive DMCA abuse complaints if you excessively abuse BitTorrents over Tor. This mostly applies if you are in the USA.

7. Create an LLC to Run Your Node- if you are operating your node at a high capacity, form an LLC or an alternative corporate entity.

Chapter 4: TrackHostExits in Tor

While browsing using Tor, you might notice that your IP address is changed more frequently. This can happen as frequently as every 3 to 5 minutes, the IP is changed. The effect will be that during your session, the server will keep on logging you out.

You may not be interested in this idea. So the only solution to this problem is to configure Tor so that the IP is only changed after amount of time that you want. You can also set it in such a way that you are the only one to change the IP and only at any time that you want. TrackHostExits are a good solution to this problem. With TrackHostExit, one can set a list of domains so that Tor should use the same exit relay for all these domains for a given amount of time. Note that this time is specified in seconds. Consider the example shown below:

TrackHostsExits.sample.org

TrackHostsExitsExpire 3600

In the above example, Tor will use the same exit relays for all subdomains of sample.org for one hour, that is, 3600 seconds. This shows how simple and quick it is to use Tor TrackHostExits.

After re-visiting certain websites from a different IP, you might be logged out. This feature relies on the LongLivedPorts. You can choose to add the following to the torrc which will establish connections to certain ports using the same circuit for a longer time:

LongLivedPorts
80,23,21,22,706,1863,5050,5190,5222,5223,6667,8300,888 8

The services identified by these ports usually have long-running connections. A good example of this is the interactive shell or the chat. Circuits for the streams using these ports usually have nodes. This helps in keeping a node high until the stream is finished. Client and server circuits, which involve hidden services with a virtual port, contained in the list also honor this. MapAddress is a good alternative to LongLivedPorts. However, this applies only to certain sites.

With this, connections to a given site will always go through the same connection. In case you need your site to be visited through a particular country, this is a good option for you. Consider the example shown below:

MapAddress www.mywebsite.com
www.mywebsite.com.node.exit

In the above example, visits to the www.mywebsite.com will only be through node. However, this should be replaced with the node that you know, including its location. Suppose that you are the only person in use of this node, this means that when connections come from the same node, www.mywebsite.com will easily know that it is the same person.

Chapter 6: EntryNodes in Tor

This is a list of nodes which are preferred for use as the first node of the circuit.

Protecting against fake entry nodes

It is possible for attackers to set up fake entry nodes and then use them to redirect your outgoing connections to them. This also applies when you have to route all the data you have through their network. The question is, what can you do prevent such cases as a Tor user and what does Tor do to prevent such things from happening?

Note that every packet either needs to be forwarded or is an exit packet. Each packet is encrypted for a specific node. Each and every node contains a public key. This key is then used for negotiation of a session key with the other node. This is called the principle of onion routing. To summarize this, understand that the packet is specifically encrypted to the last node and then the encryption is done to the second from the last node. This process is continued. Traffic analysis will be needed to link the original sender to the raw packet if every node in the chain is not controlled.

There is the publication of the public key for a Tor node. This means that in the whole chain, no node will be able to redirect your traffic in any meaningful way. Passage must be to the node with the capability of decryption. Signed Diffie-Hellman exchange is employed for the purpose of deriving a symmetric key. This means that a node which doesn't have a matching private key for the public key which has been published will not accept this. Layered encryption and key exchange prevents the removal of nodes down the chain by malicious nodes.

Chapter 7: The Routing Path in Tor

Tor relies on routing paths in order to function. By default, it keeps changing the routing path every 10 minutes. This is the default setting. However, one can change this setting so that the routing path is changed at the frequency that they want. There are two ways to do this:

1. Changing the torrc configuration file.

2. Control port signal.

The torrc file has parameters which can be changed to allow the routing path to be changed at the wanted frequency. These parameters include the following:

1. NewCircuitPeriod NUM- the default number of seconds is 30. They determine whether to build a new circuit. The new circuit is only built if necessary, otherwise it is not built. You can change the default value of 30 seconds to the one that you need.

2. MaxCircuitDirtiness NUM- it is good to reuse a circuit that was used some number of seconds ago. However, it is not advisable to attach a new stream to an old circuit. Note that this value is set to 10 minutes by default. Making this value smaller implies that the circuit will get old more often. The opposite is also true.

3. CircuitIdleTimeout NUM- if a circuit which has not been used (clean circuit) is kept idle for a few seconds (number of seconds), then it is closed. In case the Tor client is totally idle, it can expire all the circuits it has. This is

then followed by the expiration of the available TLS connections.

4. Note that this is set to a default value of 1 hour. If the circuit which is made is not good for exiting the requests which are being received, it will not take up a slot in the circuit list forever.

Since the circuits are regularly created, closing it should be done regularly too. If you need to decrease the idle time, then use this option. Note that when accessing at the same time, the circuit will not be switched. This is a disadvantage associated with this method. For you to get the right result, you have to play around with the values. The second method offers a configuration which cannot be changed. However, in case the first method above doesn't work, try to use this method. On Vidalia, there is a button labelled "Use new identity". It functions by sending a signal to the Tor's control port so that the identity can be changed. One can write a script so that the signal is sent after a desired period.

Chapter 8: Accessing Dark Internet using Tor

The dark internet, popularly known as DarkNet, is a small network within the internet. Accessing DarkNet using your browser is not easy, and cannot normally be done. The requests to DarkNet are encrypted and are not traceable and it lacks any domain names which you would aware of. In Tor, there is no .net/.com. Instead of these, it uses .onion. You can try to type it into your browser. You will see that nothing will show up. For you to access the websites forming the dark internet or the deep web, that is, hidden websites, you must do it from inside the Tor network. The dark internet contains data about everything. If you need political secrets, this is the right place to find them. If you also need to become an anonymous hacker, then this is a right place for you. People, who normally leak information, as with WikiLeaks, get it from the dark internet. Which should clearly illustrate how important the data you can get from there is. You should note that you can find fun, enjoyment, and other interesting things as well. However, it is dangerous and there are many risks involved due to the fake websites that you can also find. These can lead you to jail. If this happens, you will be held responsible for that. It is good to be keen when accessing the dark internet as something unexpected may happen. Follow the following steps:

1. Get your Mind Ready- learn more about both Tor and the dark internet before getting started. Understand that most of the information on DarkNet is illegal, so it is dangerous to take actions there at all. Hidden wiki is used to facilitate an illegal action. In most cases, they are used to providing services which are hidden through the Tor network.

2. Assemble Your Tools- you need to download the TOR bundle. This should include the browser to be used for accessing the dark internet, sockets, and the protocol. These should be dependent on the operating system that is running on your machine.

3. Access the Network- installation of the bundle is very easy, so you won't find any difficulty there. Once the process of installation is over, just start the browser. This should come with the setup. At this point, Tor should be up and running. Make sure that you have started it by clicking on "start".

4. You can then use the browser to access the websites that you need. You will even be able to access blocked websites. The proxy will help in concealing your identity meaning that you will be secure against being traced.

Chapter 9: Creating a Tor Button in Chrome

It is possible to add a Tor button in Chrome for the purpose of on-demand, anonymous browsing. Tor provides distributed and free proxies for private downloading and anonymous browsing. In Tor, there is a built-in Firefox add-on. Since it has no add-on for Chrome, it is necessary to add an on/off button for Chrome in Tor. Just follow the simple steps found below:

1. Download and install Tor on your computer. It is recommended that you download either the Mac or Windows bundle.

2. In the Chrome browser, install the Proxy Switch.

3. The "Tor" profile name should then be changed. Set the http proxy to 127.0.0.1 and the port to 8118. The box "Use the same proxy server for all protocols" should then be checked. Click on the "Save" button located at the bottom.

4. From the options of Proxy Switch, open the general tab. identifies the "Quick Switch" button and checks it. Choose "binary switch". Profile 1 should then be made "[direct connection]" while profile 2 should be made "Tor". This can also be set to the name that you used before for your profile. Save the settings by clicking on the "Save" button.

5. Use your button to switch between Tor connection and normal connection.

Before hitting the Proxy Switch button in Chrome, make sure that Tor is up and running. You might need to check whether the Chrome browser is using Tor while browsing. To do this, go to the system tray and right-click on the TOR button.

If you are using Mac, move to the status bar and click on the onion icon there. This should be followed by opening of the bandwidth monitoring tool. For testing purposes, browse to a site with images which are large. If the bandwidths for transferring with Tor moves up then you know that you are now browsing anonymously using Chrome and Tor together.

Chapter 10: Using Tor safely on Windows

Users of Tor on Windows sometimes encounter attacks while browsing. Tor is an advanced model of Firefox. The attackers are able to gain access in any browsers with Firefox-like base. It explains why you should be extra-vigilant while using Tor. This attack can be carried out on either Tor or the Tor browser. This explains why the security of the two is important rather than focusing on only one of them.

Securing only one of these will leave the other as a candidate for launching attacks which is not recommended. If you are using an old version of Tor browser, then you are highly vulnerable to attacks. You then need to do something about it since you are not secure.

What you should do

With Tor, updates cannot be downloaded and installed automatically. Instead, the user of the Tor browser must download and install the updates manually on their computer. If you are using an outdated version of Tor and you are using Windows, kindly follow the procedure below to update your Tor browser:

1. Open the Tor browser running on your computer. Identify the version of Firefox being run on your machine. Just click on the "Tor Browser" button.

2. Click on the "Help" button and determine the version of the Firefox. If the version is below 17.07, this means that you are vulnerable to attacks.

3. Click on the TorButton icon. Choose "Download Tor Browser Bundle Update".

4. You will then find yourself in the Tor Browser Bundle homepage. To download the executable file of the update, click on the "Download" button.

5. Wait for the download to complete and then save it somewhere easy to access. If you are warned about launching the executable file, just click through the warnings.

6. Once the download is over, extract in the directory of choice. You can extract to the same location it has been downloaded or into a new directory. You can also extract it into the directory where the Tor has been installed. However, this is not necessary.

7. The last step is to launch the browser. Navigate to the directory where you did the extraction of the application. Check its version to identify whether you are up-to-date. If the version of Firefox is 17.01, then you are okay.

Note this form of attack is for windows users running old versions of Tor browser. This explains why you should keep your Tor browser updated. It is recommended not to use Tor on windows, but instead, use it on other platforms such as Linux and Mac OS X.

This is a good practice to ensure your security. However, if this is not possible, then just update your browser on a regular basis and all will be well. If security is a major issue for you, then it is wise to disable JavaScript and then install the Firefox add-on called Request Policy. This will control the kind of origins loaded from any given website.

Chapter 11: Tips while using the Tor Browser

The following are tips which are necessary to ensure your security while using the Tor browser:

1. Avoid Torrents or File-Sharing- these applications usually avoid proxy and make direct connections even after being directed to use Tor.

2. Avoid Installing or Enabling Browser Plugins- these can be manipulated to reveal your IP address. They include Flash, QuickTime and RealPlayer. Also, don't try to install any other plugins or add-ons to the browser.

3. Use HTTPS Websites - this is good for encrypting privately to websites.

4. Documents which are downloaded with Tor should not be Opened while Online- in case you are warned of the same, do not ignore it.

5. Don't Connect to a Public Network Directly- rather, use a bridge or a company. This will prevent anyone from monitoring your traffic and knowing that you are using Tor.

Conclusion

It can be concluded that the Tor browser is used for anonymous web browsing, whereby the users conceal both the usage and their location from people performing traffic analysis and network surveillance.

The browser was introduced by the US Navy as a way to safely and securely use the internet. Other groups which have used the browser include whistle-blowers, reporters, and political activists. The browser works by encrypting both the data on transmission and the IP addresses. This also makes it impossible for one to know the origin or destination of the data.

To be totally secure, and especially on Windows, one needs to update the browser frequently. If you fail to do this, you will be vulnerable to attacks. JavaScript should also be uninstalled and no add-ons should be installed. The browser is updated manually.

www.ingramcontent.com/pod-product-compliance
Lightning Source LLC
Chambersburg PA
CBHW070929050326
40689CB00015B/3673